Thinking Critically: Social Networking

Andrea C. Nakaya

ReferencePoint Press®

San Diego, CA

About the Author

Andrea C. Nakaya, a native of New Zealand, holds a BA in English and an MA in communications from San Diego State University. She has written and edited numerous books on current issues. She currently lives in Encinitas, California, with her husband and their two children, Natalie and Shane.

© 2014 ReferencePoint Press, Inc.
Printed in the United States

For more information, contact:
ReferencePoint Press, Inc.
PO Box 27779
San Diego, CA 92198
www. ReferencePointPress.com

Picture Credits:
Cover credit: Thinkstock Images
Thinkstock: 9
Steve Zmina: 16, 21, 29, 35, 42, 48, 56, 62

LIBRARY OF CONGRESS CATALOGING-IN-PUBLICATION DATA

Nakaya, Andrea C., 1976-
  Thinking critically : social networking / by Andrea C. Nakaya.
    p. cm. -- (Thinking critically)
  Includes bibliographical references and index.
  ISBN-13: 978-1-60152-588-8 (hardback)
  ISBN-10: 1-60152-588-5 (hardback)
  1. Online social networks. 2. Internet and teenagers. 3. Internet--Safety measures. 4. Social media. I. Title.
  HM742.N35 2013
  006.7'54--dc23
                                                              2012043628

Contents

Foreword

"Literacy is the most basic currency of the knowledge economy we're living in today." Barack Obama (at the time a senator from Illinois) spoke these words during a 2005 speech before the American Library Association. One question raised by this statement is: What does it mean to be a literate person in the twenty-first century?

E.D. Hirsch Jr., author of *Cultural Literacy: What Every American Needs to Know*, answers the question this way: "To be culturally literate is to possess the basic information needed to thrive in the modern world. The breadth of the information is great, extending over the major domains of human activity from sports to science."

But literacy in the twenty-first century goes beyond the accumulation of knowledge gained through study and experience and expanded over time. Now more than ever literacy requires the ability to sift through and evaluate vast amounts of information and, as the authors of the Common Core State Standards state, to "demonstrate the cogent reasoning and use of evidence that is essential to both private deliberation and responsible citizenship in a democratic republic."

The Thinking Critically series challenges students to become discerning readers, to think independently, and to engage and develop their skills as critical thinkers. Through a narrative-driven, pro/con format, the series introduces students to the complex issues that dominate public discourse—topics such as gun control and violence, social networking, and medical marijuana. All chapters revolve around a single, pointed question such as Can Stronger Gun Control Measures Prevent Mass Shootings?, or Does Social Networking Benefit Society?, or Should Medical Marijuana Be Legalized? This inquiry-based approach introduces student researchers to core issues and concerns on a given topic. Each chapter includes one part that argues the affirmative and one part that argues the negative—all written by a single author. With the single-author format the predominant arguments for and against an

4

issue can be synthesized into clear, accessible discussions supported by details and evidence including relevant facts, direct quotes, current examples, and statistical illustrations. All volumes include focus questions to guide students as they read each pro/con discussion, a list of key facts, and an annotated list of related organizations and websites for conducting further research.

The authors of the Common Core State Standards have set out the particular qualities that a literate person in the twenty-first century must have. These include the ability to think independently, establish a base of knowledge across a wide range of subjects, engage in open-minded but discerning reading and listening, know how to use and evaluate evidence, and appreciate and understand diverse perspectives. The new Thinking Critically series supports these goals by providing a solid introduction to the study of pro/con issues.

Social Networking

In 2010 Kaitlin Kerry Eckrote, a student at Pennsylvania State University, posted on a class blog about her Facebook use. According to Eckrote, Facebook is an important part of her life, and she spends a significant amount of time on the website every day. She says, "I wake up in the morning . . . and turn on my computer. First thing I do is check Facebook. I go to class & when I come back I check Facebook again." Eckrote adds, "The rest of my day is spent going back and forth from doing important things to checking Facebook." Among her friends, spending so much time on Facebook is normal. She says, "I know that virtually everyone has a facebook; when someone doesn't my friends and I are often appalled."[1]

Research shows that Eckrote's experience is a common one and that social media use is an important part of life all over the world. According to research company comScore, in 2011 social networking became the most popular online activity worldwide. The company studied 2 million people in 171 countries and reports that 1.2 billion people around the world use social networking sites. As this number reveals, social networks have become an important part of society. Not only are more and more people using them, but this widespread use is changing the way people communicate and provoking intense debate about how society is being impacted.

How Social Networking Is Used

Social networking sites allow people to connect with each other for many different reasons. A large number of people use sites such as Facebook and Tumblr to connect with friends. Others use sites like LinkedIn for networking in their career field or finding a new job. Some social networking sites allow users to connect with specific groups of people with which they have something in common; for example, dating sites like Match.com allow users to find individuals who share similar interests, Flixster allows movie fans to share information about movies, and Flickr allows users to share images and videos.

In the vast majority of countries, Facebook is the leading social networking site. Launched in 2004, Facebook now has more users than any other social networking site—more than 1 billion in 2012. ComScore reports that in 2011, three of every four minutes spent on social networking sites were spent on Facebook. The research company maintains, "By and large, Facebook has proven to be a dominant global force in social networking that shows no immediate signs of slowing down."[2] Facebook also dominates in the United States. The Pew Research Center reports that 87 percent of US social networking users have a Facebook profile. Facebook does not allow users younger than age thirteen, but research shows that despite this, many children under thirteen have Facebook accounts—often with their parents' knowledge. In 2012 *Consumer Reports* reported that at least 5.6 million children using Facebook are under age thirteen.

While Facebook is the most used social networking site, there are many other popular ones. Most research shows that Twitter is the second most used site after Facebook. Other popular sites include LinkedIn, Google+, MySpace, and Tumblr. Pinterest is one of the fastest-growing sites. According to research company Experian, in 2012 it became the third-most visited social networking website. Most research about who uses social networking shows that networking is most common among young people. However, it is widely used by all age groups.

Changing the Way People Communicate

Social networking is becoming an increasingly important part of life, and this trend is expected to continue. As comScore explains, young people—who rely on this form of communication the most—are making it an integral part of society and are expected to pass this behavior on to their children in the future: "[The] data collectively suggest that much of the communication going on between 15–24 year olds happens via social networks." It predicts, "As this generation matures, carrying these highly social behaviors into the future, it is possible that social networking, or its natural successor, could become the most important communication channel across all age groups."[3]

The increasing importance of social networks is resulting in some profound changes to the way people interact. Divided attention has become commonplace. People who gather with friends or colleagues in a restaurant or meeting room are often engaged at the same time with social network updates and posts. Canadian psychology student Marisa Murray describes the experience of going to a restaurant and finding all the families seated around her completely absorbed in electronic devices rather than engaging in face-to-face conversation: "It was so strange. There was no conversation. Within the family, everyone had a cellphone. They ordered their appetizers, then they all got back to their device. There was minimal conversation among the family members." According to Murray, "The conversation that was happening was along the lines of who was updating Facebook, what they were tweeting or a game they were playing. I couldn't believe it. . . . It boggled my mind."[4]

Constant Connection

Mobile devices such as smartphones that allow people to access their social networks from wherever they are have fueled the increase in social networking. Research company Nielsen finds that among US smartphone owners who download applications, social networking is the third most used type of application after games and weather. ComScore reports that two in five smartphone owners in the United States and one in four in the European Union use their phones to access their social networks almost every day.

Whether social networking's impact on society is positive or negative is a matter for debate. On the one hand, it allows people to connect with family, friends, acquaintances, and individuals whom they might never have met in person but who share common interests. And these connections can occur regardless of geographic location and can be as few or as many as desired. On the other hand, constant connections to other people via social networks have fundamentally altered face-to-face interactions

Social networking has become an integral form of communication for people around the world. It has resulted in profound changes—some positive, some negative—in human interaction.

that were once the essence of personal relationships and human communities. Psychologist and technology expert Sherry Turkle observes, "Mobile technology has made each of us 'pauseable.' Our face-to-face conversations are routinely interrupted by incoming calls and text messages." Such behavior used to be considered extremely rude, she says, but, "in the new etiquette, turning away from those in front of you to answer a mobile phone or respond to a text has become close to the norm. When someone holds a phone, it can be hard to know if you have that person's attention."[5]

Shifting the Boundaries of Privacy

Not only is social networking changing the way people interact, it is also changing the content of those interactions. On social networking sites, people often share much more personal information with their friends than they do face-to-face. As technology expert David Kirkpatrick explains, "Facebook is causing a mass resetting of the boundaries of personal intimacy. . . . Many users willingly fill out extensive details about their career, relationships, interests, and personal history. If you are friends with someone on Facebook, you may learn more about them than you learned in ten years of offline friendship."[6]

This willingness to share personal information, coupled with the relative ease of accessing much of the information people post online, has raised concerns about threats to privacy. These concerns have at times played out in real life, as when employers turn down potential job candidates after viewing inappropriate photos or comments on social networking pages. In addition, advertisers collect huge amounts of data from social networking users and turn that information into targeted advertising for a wide array of products and services. Critics contend that by collecting and analyzing so much personal information (often without express permission of the users), the social networking sites and their business partners threaten a user's privacy.

While these types of concerns are common among industry watchers, many social network users seem much less concerned with the whole privacy issue. In this new digital age, ideas about what constitutes or threatens privacy are changing. Many people feel that the sharing of information—personal and otherwise—has created a more open, transparent society—and they like this new openness. Those who do not share these views can (and usually do) take steps to restrict access to the information they share on their social networking pages.

Considering the Effects of Social Networking

Every day, social networking gains popularity in communities all over the world, and it seems likely to be a permanent part of society's future. President Barack Obama's actions after winning reelection in 2012 reveal just how much a part of life networking already is. According to the *Los Angeles Times*, the first thing Obama did after the networks projected his win was to tweet his 23 million Twitter followers, thanking them for their support. As social networking becomes an integral part of communication, and in some cases the dominant form of communication, it will continue to have a significant impact on society, the individual, privacy, and safety. By thinking critically about these issues, users can be aware of how social networking affects them and make sure their social networking experience is what they want it to be.

Chapter One

Does Social Networking Benefit Society?

Social Networking Benefits Society

- Social networking facilitates connection between members of society.
- Networks are a valuable resource for solving problems and finding information.
- Social networking can facilitate social change.
- Critiques of social networking are based on fear and not supported by facts.

The Debate at a Glance

Social Networking Does Not Benefit Society

- Social networking causes people to disconnect from the present.
- Networking is causing more superficial communication.
- People frequently present a false self on social networks.
- Social networking can perpetuate closed-mindedness and prejudice.

Social Networking Benefits Society

"Social media can connect us with communities across the world, accelerate our understanding of complex topics, help us keep track of the ones we love, and gently remind us we are not alone."

Alyson Krokosky, Mark Petruniak, and Sharon F. Terry, "Social Media Provides Tools for Discovery: How to Find Value in Social Networking," *Exceptional Parent*, September 2011. www.eparentdigital.com.

Consider these questions as you read:

1. Do you agree that social networking enhances face-to-face socialization rather than replaces it? Why or why not?
2. Can you think of a time when you used social networking to find an answer to a question or problem? Would this problem have been more difficult to answer without the help of your network? Explain.
3. Social networks allow information to spread quickly to huge groups of people. In some cases this can have a positive impact; for example, helping facilitate social change. How might this quick spread of information also have a negative impact?

Editor's note: The discussion that follows presents common arguments made in support of this perspective, reinforced by facts, quotes, and examples taken from various sources.

Social networking benefits society by facilitating and strengthening social connection. It makes it possible to create and maintain connections with large numbers of people, including those in different geographical zones. Overall, it allows a person to have a larger group of friends and connect with them more often. Blogger Billygean writes about how social media gives her more opportunities to connect with friends than she would otherwise have. Billygean says that she still meets with her friends in person on a regular basis, but the use of social media sites allows her extra time for socializing with them. For example, not only does she have face-to-face conversations with friends, she also shares pictures with them on her social network and posts short messages on their walls. In addition, she can have conversations with her many cousins whom she would not be able to telephone regularly. She says, "Do we talk less because of social networking? No, I think we talk more."[7] Without social networking, she believes, her social life would be less rich.

Strengthening Social Connections

Sometimes, communication on social networks is more intimate precisely because it does not occur face-to-face. A person using a social network can easily share thoughts and feelings with everyone in his or her network with one status update, whereas it would be impossible to do this face-to-face with every person. For example, in a typical day one social network user might share that he or she got a new pet, finished a good book, felt happy about the rain, and found a great, new restaurant. Without social media, it would be difficult to share so much personal information with so many friends in any one day. Josh Rose, digital creative director of advertising agency Deutsch LA, likens social media to the close-knit community from the time of his grandparents, when everyone knew what was going on in everyone else's lives. He argues that social networking encourages people to communicate and share their thoughts and feelings with their friends more than they would if they had to contact each individual separately.

In addition to encouraging deeper and more personal communication, social networking helps people be more social overall. Zeynep Tufekci, a fellow at Harvard's Berkman Center for Internet and Society, argues that many aspects of society today make it increasingly difficult to maintain friendships; for example, suburbanization (where people live farther away from their friends), long working hours, and the existence of television. She believes that social networking is an important way around such obstacles, helping people connect with each other despite having less time in which to do it. She says, "All the data I've seen say that people who use social media are . . . more social offline; or that they have benefited from social media to keep in touch with people they otherwise could not; or that many people find fellows, peers and like-minded individuals they otherwise could not find." She concludes, "In other words, texting, Facebook-status updates, and Twitter conversations are not displacing face-to-face socializing—on average, they are making them stronger."[8]

A Valuable Resource

Another advantage of social networking is that because it allows users to communicate easily with a very large group of people, it can help them efficiently and easily find information, answers to problems, or simply the feeling of connection with another person. Noaf Ereiqat, who works in marketing, relates a story that illustrates this. She says, "I have made a number of new friends through both Facebook and Twitter and make them one of my prime sources of reference when I'm on the search for anything." According to Ereiqat, "Just a few months ago, I broke my heel at a conference in Deira—an area of Dubai I am not very familiar with—and posted my annoyance on Twitter (which also feeds onto my Facebook profile). Within ten minutes I had received numerous replies not only to cheer me up, but with locations of nearby shoe repairs!"[9]

> "Texting, Facebook-status updates, and Twitter conversations are not displacing face-to-face socializing—on average, they are making them stronger."[8]
>
> —Zeynep Tufekci, a fellow at Harvard's Berkman Center for Internet and Society, a research center that investigates the impact of technology on society.

Social networking gives individuals the power to be heard—which can be helpful in cases such as Ereiqat's in which she needed to repair a shoe—but it can also have much more profound impacts when it is used to disseminate more serious opinions or messages to society. Before the existence of social media, mass media and politicians were the ones with the power to reach large groups of society. But the rise of social media has changed this, allowing people who were previously unknown to become visible to the larger community. Sheryl Sandberg, chief operating officer of Facebook, says, "The strength of social media is that it empowers individuals to amplify and broadcast their voices." She says, "[It] gives a name and a face—a true identity—to those who were previously invisible, and it turns up the volume on voices that may have otherwise been too soft to hear."[10]

A Tool for Social Change

Because it allows individual viewpoints to be heard and quickly spread to huge groups of people, social networking can be a powerful tool for social change. Ideas often spread expo-nentially—as when one person posts an opinion or experience and then his or her contacts share that post-ing with their friends, who then pass it on to their friends, and so on. Such widespread sharing of ideas can have a powerful effect and even lead to social change. Technology expert David Kirk-patrick calls this the Facebook Effect. It can happen unintentionally, when people simply share their thoughts and feelings on their social networks. But individuals can also use social networking as a purposeful tool to spread information and ideas. Net-working is a very powerful tool. Explains Kirkpatrick, "Ideas on Face-book have the ability to rush through groups and make many people aware of something almost simultaneously, spreading from one person to another and on to many with unique ease—like a virus."[11]

> "The strength of social media is that it empowers individuals to amplify and broadcast their voices."[10]
>
> —Sheryl Sandberg, chief operating officer of the social networking website Facebook.

Many people argue that Facebook and Twitter played an important role in a revolution that occurred in Egypt in 2011, a response to years of repression and corruption by the Egyptian government. Facebook's role began when twenty-nine-year-old Wael Ghonim found images of Khaled Mohamed Said, a man who had been beaten to death by Egyptian police. He created a Facebook page called "Kullena Khaled Said," meaning, "We Are All Khaled Said," which called for an end to the government's corrup-tion. According to the *New York Times*, within two minutes of his starting the page, 30 people had joined, and after three months more than 250,000 had joined. More and more people joined via Facebook and Twitter, rais-ing awareness and organizing large protests, and in less than seven months, the country overthrew its government. Ghonim believes Facebook was a

Networking Is a Valuable Social Tool

Social networking is beneficial because it facilitates and strengthens social connections. This graph shows the many ways people use social networking to enhance their social lives. It reveals that a large percentage use it to stay in touch with friends and family members and to connect with old friends. A smaller percentage use networking to connect with others who share similar interests and to make new friends.

Motivations for using social networking sites
Based on adults who use social networking sites such as Facebook, MySpace, LinkedIn, and/or Twitter

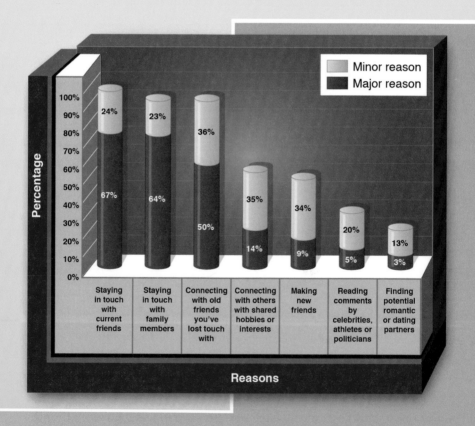

very important part of the revolution because it allowed people to communicate and coordinate. He says, "This revolution started—well, a lot of this revolution started on Facebook. If you want to liberate a society, just give them the Internet. If you want to have a free society, just give them Internet."[12]

Beneficial Overall

Negative critiques of social media are a result of fear and ignorance of this technology. History repeatedly shows that when a new technology comes into widespread use, it is human nature to be suspicious of it. This happened with the printing press, television, and the telephone. When the telephone was invented, many feared it would result in people going out less because they would stay at home and have their conversations on the telephone. Yet just as the telephone did not destroy society, neither will social networking. Like the telephone and the printing press, social networking will change society, but the overall effect will be beneficial. Rose argues that in the face of new technology people often focus on their fear of change instead of recognizing what they are gaining. He says, "I think very often, we lament what we miss and forget to admire what we've become."[13]

He shares the way that social networking helps him stay close with his ten-year-old son who does not live with him all the time. Rose explains that because of networking, they can communicate small pieces of information such as what they are eating for breakfast or what they have planned for the day, and this helps them feel closer to each other. He maintains that while this form of communication might not be ideal, their relationship is better because of it. Says Rose, "Is it better than a conversation with 'real words?' No. But is it much better than waiting two more days, when the mundane moment that I long to hear about so much is gone? Yes."[14] Overall, social networking technology has benefited society. It allows people to connect with one another more frequently and more intimately than before. It is also a valuable tool for finding information and spreading ideas. With social networking, society has gained a powerful tool to enhance and control its communication.

Social Networking Does Not Benefit Society

"Within this world of instant and absolute communication, unbounded by limits of time or space, we suffer from unprecedented alienation. We have never been more detached from one another, or lonelier."

Stephen Marche, "Is Facebook Making Us Lonely?," *Atlantic*, May 2012. www.theatlantic.com.

Consider these questions as you read:

1. How persuasive is the argument that social networking causes people to disconnect from the present? Which arguments provide the strongest support for this perspective, and why?
2. In your experience, how does communication on social networks differ from face-to-face communication? Which form of communication do you like better, and why?
3. Some people argue that it does not matter whether the 2012 video about Joseph Kony resulted in groupthink, because it still had the desired effect of raising public awareness about Kony and his crimes. Do you agree or disagree? Explain.

Editor's note: The discussion that follows presents common arguments made in support of this perspective, reinforced by facts, quotes, and examples taken from various sources.

Social networking causes people to disconnect from the present, resulting in a decreased sense of community. People often become obsessed with their network friends, many of whom they have never met. At the same time they give less attention to friends, coworkers, neighbors, and others they see daily, and they put less effort into developing personal relationships. Networking psychologist and technology expert Sherry Turkle argues that when people use social networks, they check out of their current reality—meaning they are less likely to engage in face-to-face interaction. For instance, she says, "at a café a block from my home, almost everyone is on a computer or smartphone as they drink their coffee." Before the existence of social networking, some of these people might have been talking to one another rather than communicating via computer. Turkle says she feels lonely because, as a result of their focus on computers and other devices, these people are not really present in the same space as she is. She has lost some of her sense of community with those around her. She says, "These people are not my friends, yet somehow I miss their presence."[15]

Detracting from Quality Communication

Even when people spend time together, social networking often detracts from those experiences. It is now common, for example, for a person to interrupt a face-to-face conversation to read or post a status update on a social network via a mobile device. In an online forum about social networking, one respondent comments, "From personal experience, I have seen the quality of interaction from my network-submersed friends decline greatly. For them, network always trumps community. Deep conversations are no longer possible since any ping from their network device requires their immediate attention."[16] Many social network users admit that the networks dominate their time and thoughts. Writer and student Denise Morris, for example, says, "When I am out and about with my friends, I grab my iPhone and check my Facebook. Whenever I see something cool or hear a funny quote or notice something quirky, I snap a photo and upload, or I post a link, or I update my status." Morris says, "I've started thinking about pictures of myself in terms of whether or not they are profile picture worthy."[17]

While this focus on social media above all else is common, research shows that many people dislike it. According to Common Sense Media, in a national study of thirteen- to seventeen-year-olds, 21 percent of teenagers wish their parents would spend less time using cell phones and other devices, and almost half say they get frustrated with their friends for using cell phones and mobile devices to do things such as check social networking sites when they are together. Common Sense quotes one sixteen-year-old respondent as saying, "I miss the times where we could just go hang out and laugh."[18] Another respondent says, "Sometimes it's nice to just sit back and relax with no possible way to communicate with anyone in any way. That's why I occasionally 'lose' my cellphone."[19]

Less Meaningful Communication

While social networking enhances quantity (how many people an individual can connect with), it dilutes the quality of communication. In essence, it encourages superficial relationships. Communicating online is different from face-to-face communication because it does not allow a participant to see actions or reactions. Before posting anything online, each participant in the conversation has the ability to think about—and edit—what they present. As journalist Stephen Marche argues, "It enables us to be social while sparing us the embarrassing reality of society—the accidental revelations we make at parties, the awkward pauses, the farting and the spilled drinks."[20] This form of interaction is often more superficial because it has been edited. While most people do not enjoy the embarrassing moments, experiencing these things can help people better understand one another and make their relationships deeper and stronger.

Not only is online communication frequently edited for content, it is often edited in length. Turkle explains how communication on social networks is likely to become more brief and simplified. She says, "Face-to-face conversation unfolds slowly. It teaches patience." In contrast, she says, "when we communicate on our digital devices, we learn different habits. As we ramp up the volume and velocity of online connections, we start to expect faster answers. To get these, we ask one another simpler questions; we dumb down our communications, even on the most important matter."[21] She argues that while face-to-face communication takes more time and effort than this simplified online communication, it is more rewarding and builds stronger relationships.

Just as social networking encourages people to engage in more edited conversations, it also encourages them to present a more edited, and often less truthful, online persona. Users of social networking

Social Networking Disrupts Friendships

A 2012 survey of 1,030 teenagers, aged thirteen to seventeen, finds that many teens feel frustrated by the demands of social networking and the effect it has on friendships. One teen participant commented that her close friendships have dwindled as her friends have become absorbed by social networking. This sentiment is reflected in the percentage of respondents who expressed frustration with friends for texting or social networking when they were spending time together.

Among all 13- to 17-year-olds, the percentage who say they strongly or somewhat agree that they:	
Get frustrated with friends for texting or social networking when hanging out together	45%
Wish they could unplug for a while sometimes	43%
Sometimes wish they could go back to a time when there was no Facebook	36%
Wish their parents spent less time with cell phones and other devices	21%

Source: Common Sense Media, "Social Media, Social Life: How Teens View Their Digital Lives," Summer 2012. www.commonsensemedia.org.

sites do not usually share *all* of their thoughts, feelings, and photos with friends. Instead they select certain ones, thus presenting a view of themselves that might not be entirely accurate. While people routinely edit what they say about themselves in face-to-face conversation, too, it is much easier to create an image online than in person. Because users are interacting through a computer or phone, they have time to consider what they say, and they have the opportunity to say it without anyone actually seeing them.

New Media Age magazine argues that in social networking, people are constantly thinking about how others will perceive their comments and actions, and as a result they edit what they present, often resulting in a false self on their networks. The magazine says, "We're more worried about our personal brands than the absolute truth." Referring specifically to Facebook and its founder, Mark Zuckerberg, it argues, "Facebook's terms state that users 'will not provide any false personal information.' Yet in forcing people to interact using their real names, its creating a web of falseness, a Zuckerberg production of correctness, airbrushed photos and sanitization."[22] As a result, communication among friends on social networks such as Facebook is less meaningful because they are not revealing their true selves to each other.

> ## "[Facebook is] creating a web of falseness, a Zuckerberg production of correctness, airbrushed photos and sanitization."[22]
>
> —New Media Age, a UK publication that provides news about interactive media.

Pulitzer Prize–winning columnist Connie Schultz writes about people who edit their social networking personas by never posting negative or unhappy things about themselves, and she admits to being one of them. She says, "A lot of people are so relentlessly happy it's annoying. People like me, I'm suddenly realizing." She reveals that on Facebook, "I never have admitted to having a really bad day. I was raised to be sunny no matter how dark the skyline. In a land of Eeyores, I'm Tigger."[23] Yet Schultz wonders whether this false presentation of constant happiness actually encourages phony relationships.

Groupthink

Some people argue that social networking benefits society by helping to spread a variety of new ideas; however, in many cases the opposite is true. A social network can just as easily perpetuate a single or narrow point of view. This happens when people blindly go along with the dominant point of view being espoused on the network and do not consider alternatives. For example, if the majority of a person's network friends read and repost an article arguing that a particular politician is dishonest, then that person might simply go along with the opinion because he or she has read it so many times and has not been exposed to any other way of thinking, or the person does not want to be different from his or her friends. Psychologists call this "groupthink."

An example of groupthink in social networking occurred in 2012, when charity organization Invisible Children released a video about Joseph Kony. Kony is the alleged leader of the Lord's Resistance Army (LRA), a militant group in Uganda that is responsible for kidnapping, killing, and mutilating thousands of people. In 2005 the International Criminal Court (ICC) issued a warrant for his arrest. Invisible Children's 2012 video sought to raise awareness about Kony and bring him to justice, a goal that many people believe is good. However, large numbers of people liked and reposted the Kony video without even being aware of the facts related to Kony or Invisible Children. (The organization has since been accused of manipulating facts and misusing funds.) As one blogger states, "Most people who have either liked or reposted the video are hardly aware of the facts that relate to the LRA, their uprising, and the role of the ICC. One person I spoke to, who avidly reposted and commented ferociously on the video, could not even restate what the ICC acronym stood for; she could only recite that Kony was a bad person that needed to be brought to justice and the only way to do so would be by sharing the video."[24] As this reveals, it can be easy for social networkers to engage in groupthink.

> "We live in an accelerating contradiction: the more connected we become, the lonelier we are."[25]
>
> —Stephen Marche, an author and journalist who writes a column for *Esquire* magazine.

Harming Society

Overall, social networks are having a harmful impact on society. While many people believe that networking is allowing them to become more connected to friends and more informed about the world, the opposite is actually true. As social networking proliferates, friendships and communication are becoming more edited and superficial. As Marche argues, "We live in an accelerating contradiction: the more connected we become, the lonelier we are."[25]

Chapter Two

Does Social Networking Have a Positive Impact on the Individual?

Social Networking Has a Positive Impact on the Individual

- Social networking facilitates social interaction.
- Most people report that social networking is a positive experience for them.
- Social media help socially awkward people gain confidence.
- Networking helps people connect with similar interest groups.

The Debate at a Glance

Social Networking Does Not Have a Positive Impact on the Individual

- Social networking is addicting.
- Networking can result in depression and reduced self-esteem.
- Social media use is correlated with numerous negative behaviors.
- Continual social connection does not allow youth the solitude they need for normal development.

Social Networking Has a Positive Impact on the Individual

"While there are risks inherent in online social networking, there are also many potential benefits. Social networking can provide opportunities for new relationships as well as strengthening existing relationships."

Parent Further, "Benefits of Online Social Networking," 2012. www.parentfurther.com.

Consider these questions as you read:

1. Taking into account the facts and ideas presented in this discussion, how persuasive is the argument that social networking is a positive experience for most people? What are the most persuasive facts and ideas presented?

2. Social networking allows people to have hundreds of friends and communicate with them on a regular basis. Do you think that having such a large number of friends is beneficial? Explain your answer.

3. Do you think educators should increase their use of social networking as a tool in the classroom? Why or why not?

Editor's note: The discussion that follows presents common arguments made in support of this perspective, reinforced by facts, quotes, and examples taken from various sources.

Social networking is a valuable tool that facilitates social interaction, helping individuals create new friendships and strengthen existing ones. In the days before social networking, the number of friends a person could have was often constrained by time—many people just did not have the time to maintain large numbers of friends. Now people can have hundreds of friends, because social networking technology gives them the ability to interact with all these people. In 2012 the British newspaper *Guardian* asked people how social media impacts their lives. One respondent, Kathy Gill, explained how she uses it to strengthen her friendships and interact with people she could not otherwise communicate with on a regular basis. She says, "Facebook is . . . the only place where I can comfort a niece who's having boyfriend problems; celebrate birthdays and weddings from the other side of the country; update friends and family about my life with one post that everyone can read; and easily share photos of our nephews' piano recital with grandparents living in the southwest." According to Gill, "In this digital space, I do not feel like I'm thousands of miles away."[26]

Research by the Pew Research Center shows that people who use social networking are generally better off socially, with more and stronger friendships overall. In 2011 it reported a number of statistics to back this up. For example, of those people who do not use the Internet, about 15 percent report having no close confidants with whom they can discuss important matters, while only 5 percent of social network users have no close confidants. People who use Facebook several times a day have about 9 percent more close relationships in their overall social network than those who do not use Facebook. Social network users also report higher levels of social support than non–network users. Overall, Pew says, "the average user of a social networking site has more close ties and is half as likely to be socially isolated as the average American."[27]

> "The average user of a social networking site has more close ties and is half as likely to be socially isolated as the average American."[27]
>
> —Pew Research Center, a nonpartisan organization that provides information about attitudes and trends in the United States and the world.

A Positive Experience for Most People

A number of surveys show that among people using social networking, the majority report it to be a positive experience. Common Sense Media, an organization that works to educate families about the media they consume, conducted a national study of thirteen- to seventeen-year-olds. It found that most teenagers believe social networking has a positive impact on their emotional well-being. Many of the teens who took part in the study believe social networking makes them less shy and more confident and also helps them feel better about themselves. Many also believe it has helped their relationships with both friends and family. Common Sense Media concludes that social networking is a positive experience for most teens. It says, "Despite our concerns about social media, in the vast majority of cases, these media do not appear to be causing great tumult in teenagers' lives. . . . For all the difficult stories we've heard about teens whose social lives have been turned upside down by something negative that happened online, it is good to know that only 4% of teens say that, on balance, social media has had a negative impact on their relationships with their friends."[28] Research on adults yields similar results, with the majority reporting that social networking is a positive experience for them.

Networking Builds Confidence

For people who are socially awkward, social networking can enhance confidence and communication skills and help them become more social. Some people have difficulty communicating face-to-face, and social networking can allow them to be more social than they would be in person because they can communicate online instead. Blogger SarahMummy explains that she is more comfortable communicating through social networking. She says, "I find writing easier than talking. I can say what I like and people have the option of whether they 'listen' or not. I don't feel awkward. I am funnier when I write than when I talk." She explains that communicating online is not a way to pretend to be something she is not; rather, it is a way to avoid the discomfort she sometimes feels in face-to-face-communication. She says, "I'm not hiding behind anything. I'm not pretending to be something I'm not. I'm just a little bit shy."[29] In addition to allowing socially awkward people to communicate more than they might otherwise, communicating through social media strengthens overall communication skills. This can help a shy person eventually become more comfortable in face-to-face communication.

Commenting on one online article about social networking, Danika Gusmeroli gives an example of Facebook helping an autistic girl who was socially awkward. She says, "I had a girl in my homeroom who had autism and had trouble talking to people. She had the ability to remember a lot of information but did not have the social skills and had trouble finding friends at school." According to Gusmeroli, the girl created a Facebook account, with very beneficial results:

> The high school kids took a while to warm up to the idea that she had facebook, and instead of readily accepting her facebook requests, it took a while for them to finally accept. But like a chain reaction effect, once one person accepted, so did another and another. Facebook gave her the chance to for the first time be like any other kid at high school—share photos, upload music, comment on other people's status and create status updates.[30]

Without social media, this girl might have gone through high school without experiencing the pleasure of this socialization with friends.

A Useful Tool

Even for those people who are not socially awkward, social networking can help build friendships that might not happen otherwise by helping them connect with people who share similar interests. Many social networks allow people to create or search for groups based on particular interests or affiliations. For example, Facebook has thousands of special-interest groups, including many dedicated to specific musicians, sports, types of food, and hobbies. Even the most unique interests often have a Facebook page; for example, "Green Bell Peppers Must Die!," for people who hate green bell peppers, and "People Who Always Have to Spell Their Names for Other People," for people with hard-to-spell names.

Without networks, it can be difficult for people to find others who share their particular interests, especially if they live in an area with a small population. Networking allows them to find these people with a simple search and to interact with them even if they live in different parts of the world. Blogger Karen Ballum talks about how important social networking is to her and her friends in making connections with others. She says, "It used to be that we'd have to head out in our actual physical community and attempt to find the people with the same interests as us. Sometimes it worked, sometimes it didn't." Now, says

People Feel Good about Social Networking

According to Pew Research Center surveys, significant percentages of teens and adults who engage in social networking report that it results in positive experiences for them. Specifically, it makes them feel good about themselves and enhances their relationships with other people.

Percentage of social networking site–using adults and teens who have had these experiences because of things that happened on social networking sites

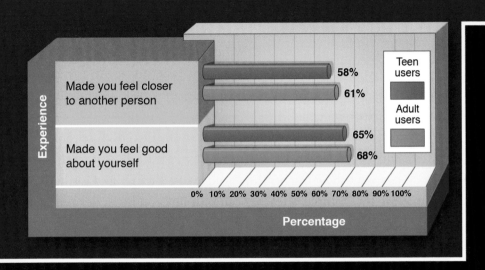

Source: Pew Research, "The Tone of Life on Social Networking Sites," February 9, 2012. http://pewinternet.org.

Ballum, social networks allow them access to a much larger group of people and increase their chances of finding others who share similar interests. She says, "I've also seen my friends turn to the internet to find their communities. Maybe they found their fellow television show fans. Or other people dealing with infertility or loss. I've seen friends turn to the internet for the support that they could not find in their own friends and communities."[31]

Social networks are also a useful tool for education. Many teachers insist that networks can be used to engage students and inspire discussion and collaboration, and a growing number of educators are using them in the classroom. British teacher Matt Britland argues that social media is effective because students already use it so much and are comfortable with it. For many students, it is their preferred method of communication. "I think it's important to embrace social media as it is the primary way that young people communicate, alongside text messaging and instant messaging," Britland says. "Much of the time we force students down the route of email. Do we do that because it is easier for us? In my experience of using Facebook groups with students they pick up communications far quicker than email."[32]

Some educators use existing social networks such as Facebook and Twitter, and others have created networks specifically for their own school. Networks allow teachers and students to quickly and easily share information; for example, a teacher can post links on his or her page and every student following that page will instantly get this information. Social media can also engage more people in discussions because it is less intimidating to speak up online than in the classroom. In-class discussions are often dominated by a small number of outspoken students, whereas online ones are more likely to include others as well.

An Invaluable Asset

Social networking is an invaluable asset that benefits the individual in myriad ways. It helps people connect and socialize in ways that were impossible before the creation of online social media, allowing them to have stronger friendships and greater numbers of friends. It is also a valuable tool for educators, the socially awkward, and those with unique interests, inspiring and facilitating communication in a continually increasing number of ways.

Social Networking Does Not Have a Positive Impact on the Individual

"Humans are social creatures; we need relationships in order to flourish. But for many, social media does not fulfill the promise of connection. That promise is best fulfilled in face-to-face conversations and relationships, rather than on Facebook."

Michael W. Austin, "Facebook Addiction?," *Psychology Today*, February 20, 2012. www.psychologytoday.com.

Consider these questions as you read:

1. Research has shown that social networking can be addictive. How does this finding compare with your own experience of social networking?
2. Can you think of a time when social networking made you feel unhappy? Why did it have this effect?
3. Do you agree with the argument that having time alone is an important part of teen development? Why or why not?

Editor's note: The discussion that follows presents common arguments made in support of this perspective, reinforced by facts, quotes, and examples taken from various sources.

Social networking has many negative effects, and its overall impact on the individual is harmful. One major problem is that networking is addictive. Many people experience the desire to constantly check their social networking sites and find it very difficult to stop themselves from doing so. A number of research studies confirm this. For example, in 2010 the International Center for Media & the Public Agenda and the Salzburg Academy of Media & Global Change conducted a study of almost one thousand students in ten countries. In that study, students were asked to abstain from using all media, including social networking sites, for a day. Researchers found strong evidence of addiction, with four in five students experiencing significant distress when they did not use their media devices and a majority unable to avoid using them. According to the researchers, "Students around the world repeatedly used the term 'addiction' to speak about their dependence on [social] media. *'Media is my drug; without it I was lost,'* said one student from Britain. *'I am an addict. How could I survive 24 hours without it?'* Sharing analogies and metaphors made explicit the depths of their distress and likened their reactions to feelings of a drug withdrawal. As a student from the USA noted: *'I was itching, like a crackhead, because I could not use my phone.'"*[33]

Small Bursts of Excitement

Journalist and 2010 Pulitzer Prize winner Matt Richtel writes about why social networking can become so addictive. Richtel explains that the human brain is programmed to stop what it is doing and respond to immediate threats or opportunities that are presented. When a person's phone or computer constantly buzzes with social networking updates, the brain can perceive these as potential threats or opportunities and is programmed to drop everything else and respond immediately. These small bursts of excitement can be addicting, writes Richtel, and people find it difficult to disconnect because they want that excitement all the time.

> "Students around the world repeatedly used the term 'addiction' to speak about their dependence on [social] media."[33]
>
> —The International Center for Media & the Public Agenda and the Salzburg Academy of Media & Global Change, organizations that do media research.

Even if the constant connection interferes with their lives, many people do not disconnect because they are addicted.

Richtel relates the story of the Campbell family of California, whose members all have trouble completely disengaging from their digital devices—to the point that it changes their lives and harms their family relationships. He says, "For spring break, the family rented a cottage in Carmel, Calif. Mrs. Campbell hoped everyone would unplug." However, reports Richtel, "Their first [night] on vacation, 'We didn't go out to dinner,' Mrs. Campbell mourned. 'We just sat there on our devices.'"[34] Yet despite wishing her family would unplug, Mrs. Campbell also finds herself drawn to her digital devices.

32

According to Richtel, "Recently, she was baking peanut butter cookies for Teacher Appreciation Day when her phone chimed in the living room. She answered a text, then became lost in Facebook, forgot about the cookies and burned them. She started a new batch, but heard the phone again, got lost in messaging, and burned those too. Out of ingredients and shamed, she bought cookies at the store."[35]

Depression and Reduced Self-Esteem

While many people find themselves unable to stay off their social networking sites, researchers have found that using those sites can actually reduce self-esteem and make people feel depressed. One reason for this is that social networking sites amplify comparisons between people—what they are doing, how many friends they have, how they look in photos—because it is displayed for everyone to see. Such public comparisons can make people less satisfied with their own lives. In an online article about the benefits of deleting one's social networking page, one person talks about how Facebook often made her feel unhappy. She says, "I found that with Facebook, I was constantly looking for thumbs up and comments, so I would work really hard to make my life either sound humorous or exciting, or whatever. And I didn't like it. There were days where none of my 150+ friends would like or comment on a status, and that made me feel like crap."[36]

Teenagers, who often struggle with insecurity and issues of self-esteem, are especially vulnerable to these sorts of feelings. Having such personal struggles publicly displayed on social media sites can be difficult and hurtful. *New York Times Magazine* staff writer Susan Dominus says, "Who has more 'friends'? Whose status update is getting more 'likes'? It's all out there for everyone to see."[37]

Journalist Jenna Wortham talks about how social networking sites can make even a normally happy person unhappy with what they are doing simply because they are afraid their friends might be doing something better. She explains how this happened to her. Says Wortham, "One recent night, I curled up on my couch with popcorn and Netflix Instant, ready to spend a quiet night at home. The peace was sweet." However, she says, "Soon, my iPhone began flashing with notifications . . . about what my friends were doing." The result: "Suddenly, my simple domestic pleasures paled in comparison with the things I could be doing."[38]

Another way social networking can be harmful to self-esteem is the fact that it is a permanent record. Even if a user deletes a post, there is frequently a copy of it recorded elsewhere. This means that everything said on a social network is displayed there permanently, including any unkind or regretted comments, any mistakes or unflattering photos. When someone makes an unkind or embarrassing remark in person, it is eventually forgotten, but online postings never go away. Says Dominus, "Every 'like' to a cruel comment, every failed attempt at humor on someone's wall—on Facebook, they live forever."[39]

Social Networking Linked to Negative Behaviors

In addition to threatening self-esteem, there is evidence that social networking can harm teens in other ways. A number of studies correlate networking with many negative behaviors, including alcohol and drug use and poor academic performance. For example, in a 2012 study of 219 students at Ohio State University, researchers found that 68 percent of those who used Facebook had significantly lower grade point averages than those who did not. In 2011 the United Kingdom's National Literacy Trust reported the results of a survey of eighteen thousand schoolchildren in England, Wales, Scotland, and Northern Ireland that suggest that social networking may be contributing to a reduction in reading. The organization reports that one in six children rarely read books outside the classroom. Instead, they prefer social networking sites and other online reading.

> "Every 'like' to a cruel comment, every failed attempt at humor on someone's wall—on Facebook, they live forever."[39]
>
> —Susan Dominus, a staff writer for the *New York Times Magazine*.

In addition to this evidence of reduced academic performance, some studies show a relationship between social networking and substance abuse. For example, according to a 2012 study by the National Center on Addiction and Substance Abuse at Columbia University, social networking is correlated with a greater likelihood of using drugs or alcohol. The study concluded that teens who see pictures of other teens using these substances often believe they are having a good time

Social Networking and Other Media Are Addicting

Social networking negatively impacts the individual because it is very addicting. This is revealed in a 2010 study of almost one thousand students in ten countries, by the International Center for Media & the Public Agenda and the Salzburg Academy of Media & Global Change. Students were asked to abstain from using all media, including social networking sites, for a day. This graph shows that significant percentages of students felt addicted to media, and felt distressed, bored, and confused without it. A significant percentage also recognized the benefits of unplugging from media.

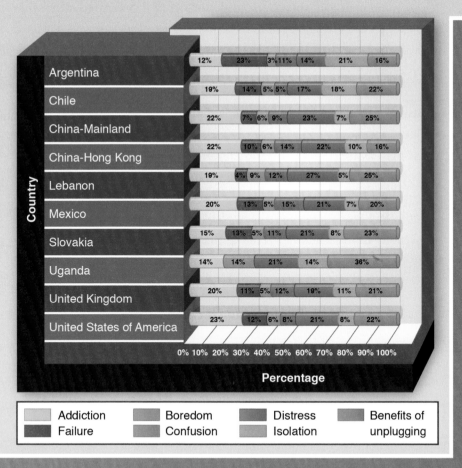

Country	Addiction	Boredom	Distress	Failure	Confusion	Isolation	Benefits of unplugging
Argentina	12%	23%	3%	11%	14%	21%	16%
Chile	19%	14%	5%	5%	17%	18%	22%
China-Mainland	22%	7%	6%	9%	23%	7%	25%
China-Hong Kong	22%	10%	6%	14%	22%	10%	16%
Lebanon	19%	4%	9%	12%	27%	5%	25%
Mexico	20%	13%	5%	15%	21%	7%	20%
Slovakia	15%	13%	5%	11%	21%	8%	23%
Uganda	14%	14%		21%	14%		36%
United Kingdom	20%	11%	5%	12%	19%	11%	21%
United States of America	23%	12%	6%	8%	21%	8%	22%

Percentage

Legend: Addiction, Failure, Boredom, Confusion, Distress, Isolation, Benefits of unplugging

Source: The World Unplugged, "Going 24 Hours Without Media," 2011. http://theworldunplugged.wordpress.com.

and want to try the same. The center found that teens who have seen pictures on social networking sites of other teens who are drunk, passed out, or using drugs are four times more likely to have used marijuana and more than three times more likely to have used alcohol.

A Lack of Solitude

Finally, some experts fear that being constantly connected to friends via social networks may be harmful to teens' development. The teenage years are a time of tremendous change and personal development. Many people believe an important part of that development is spending time alone. Yet with the creation of social networking and the ability to access networks from anywhere, some teenagers spend very little time truly alone. Even when they are physically alone, they are not really alone because they remain connected to their group of friends via social networks. Psychologist and technology expert Sherry Turkle points out that teens can be constantly engaged with their friends, from the moment they wake up until they fall asleep at night. She asks, "When is downtime, when is stillness?"[40] She quotes sixteen-year-old Julia, who communicates with her friends constantly. Julia says, "'If I'm upset, right as I feel upset, I text a couple of my friends . . . just because I know that they'll be right there and they can comfort me. If something exciting happens, I know that they'll be there to be excited with me."[41] As a result of this lack of downtime and stillness, Turkle argues that teens do not get the opportunity to think and reflect about themselves, to learn to deal with situations by themselves, or even just to be comfortable with being alone.

A Dangerous Technology

Research company A.C. Nielsen reports that Americans spend more time on Facebook than they do on any other website. And Facebook is only one of the many social networking websites used in the United States. Americans and people all over the world spend a huge amount of time using social networking, and this networking does not occur without affecting them. Unfortunately, many of these effects are negative. Social networking can be addicting and can cause depression and numerous negative behaviors. Overall, it has a harmful impact on the individual.

Chapter Three

Is Social Networking a Threat to Privacy?

Social Networking Is a Threat to Privacy

- Content posted on social media can be viewed by anyone.
- Social media sites allow people to know too much information about strangers.
- Employers infringe on privacy by researching applicants on social media.
- Social networking websites collect huge amounts of personal data on their users.

The Debate at a Glance

Social Networking Is Not a Threat to Privacy

- Social networking is changing the way people feel about privacy.
- Many people want to share their personal information with the public.
- Social media fosters openness, which benefits society in many ways.
- Sharing information publicly increases transparency and accountability.

Social Networking Is a Threat to Privacy

"Privacy, as we've known it for years, has ceased to exist."

Alex Priest, "Big Social Media on Campus," in *The Big Book of Social Media: Case Studies, Stories, Perspectives,* ed. Robert Fine. Tulsa, OK: Yorkshire, 2010, p. 102.

Consider these questions as you read:

1. Social networks allow people to view the personal information of strangers. Do you think this threatens personal privacy? Why or why not?
2. Teacher Ashley Payne was fired from her job after posting pictures of herself with alcohol on her social network. Do you think the school was justified in firing Payne? Explain your answer.
3. Taking into account the facts and ideas presented in this discussion, how persuasive is the argument that social networking is a threat to privacy? How does this perspective differ from your own?

Editor's note: The discussion that follows presents common arguments made in support of this perspective, reinforced by facts, quotes, and examples taken from various sources.

When someone posts a comment or picture on their social network, they lose control over who sees that content. Even if a person sets their privacy controls to allow only friends to see their post, the information can still end up being seen by anyone. For example, if a friend copies that information, they can pass it on to others, and many social networking websites share personal information with third-party sites for advertising purposes. Michelle Boykins from the National Crime Prevention Council warns, "One of the biggest mistakes that teens make is believing that the information that they post is private and just amongst their friends."[42] Boykins and other experts stress that people should remember that social networking sites are a public forum, even if all of the information posted

38

appears to be only between friends. Knowing this, the rule of thumb is to never post anything a person would not want to be made public.

In 2009 Georgia public high school teacher Ashley Payne was reminded of this fact. She posted vacation pictures on her Facebook page, with her privacy settings set to only her closest friends. Yet shortly after her posting, the school where she worked forced her to resign from her job after someone else viewed the photos—which showed her with alcohol—and made a complaint to her school. Payne argues that there was nothing inappropriate about her sharing these photos with her adult friends and that they were not intended to be shared with her students. However, despite her intentions, these photos were viewed by people other than her adult friends. Payne took her case to the county superior court, but it ruled against her.

> "One of the biggest mistakes that teens make is believing that the information that they post is private and just amongst their friends."[42]
>
> —Michelle Boykins, director of communications and marketing at the National Crime Prevention Council.

Viewing the Personal Information of Strangers

The way social networking sites are set up often allows users to see a lot of personal information about people they have never even met. Journalist Jenna Wortham relates the story of Tyson Balcomb, who walked into an elevator one day and realized just how much personal information Facebook allows people to see. Balcomb "found himself standing next to a woman he had never met—yet through Facebook he knew what her older brother looked like, that she was from a tiny island off the coast of Washington and that she had recently visited the Space Needle in Seattle."[43] He knew all this because they had Facebook friends in common. Says Balcomb, "I thought, maybe this is a little unhealthy."[44] Critics believe that the fact that strangers are able to view so much personal information on a social network is a threat to personal privacy.

Friends of friends are not the only ones who can view personal information posted on social networking sites. Employers report that they commonly look at potential job applicants' social networking pages as part of their consideration of whether to hire them. Insurers and college admissions officers also research candidates through social networking pages. *Consumer Reports* explains some of the things these groups look for:

> They may, for example, turn to a service such as Social Intelligence that scours public postings on Facebook and other social networks as part of a background check. Among the red flags that employers look for, the company says, are sexually explicit photos or videos, racist remarks, and evidence of illegal activities. It also reports that 69 percent of human-resource officers have rejected job applicants based on social media reviews that turned up any of these activities.[45]

Some companies go even further and ask potential employees for their social media passwords in order to check their pages.

Many people believe this kind of research is a threat to privacy. They argue that social networking sites are intended to be private discussions among friends and that even though employers and insurers might have the ability to access this information, to do so is an infringement of privacy. Some states have recently taken action toward restricting this access. According to the National Conference of State Legislatures, in 2012 fourteen states introduced legislation that would restrict employers from requesting information that would allow them to access the social networking sites of applicants, students, or employees. As of this writing, California, Maryland, and Illinois had passed legislation that prohibits employers from requesting or requiring an applicant or employee to provide their social media user name or password. In California and Delaware, legislation was enacted that prohibits colleges and universities from requesting account information from students.

Collecting User Data

Employers are not the only ones using social media to collect information about people. Social networking sites collect large amounts of data about their users. According to journalist Mark Sullivan, collecting and selling personal information is a huge and growing market, one that many people are unaware of, even though most people are affected by it. He explains:

When you update your Facebook page, "Like" something on a website, apply for a credit card, click on an ad, listen to an MP3, or comment on a YouTube video, you are feeding a huge and growing beast with an insatiable appetite for your personal data, a beast that always craves more. Virtually every piece of personal information that you provide online (and much that you provide offline) will end up being bought and sold, segmented, packaged, analyzed, repackaged, and sold again.[46]

According to Sullivan, the people buying and selling this data include marketers, advertisers, data brokers, online tracking companies, and website publishers. An example of the way this data is used is a program that tracks a person's web browsing then sends targeted advertising based on the types of web pages he or she has been viewing.

Facebook's Data Collection Practices Scrutinized

In 2012, *Consumer Reports* investigated privacy and social networks. It focused on Facebook, the largest social network in the world, and found many causes for concern. The organization cautions that most people do not realize exactly how much personal information is being collected about them or the number of people who can access that information. It says that many Facebook users do not use privacy controls, with approximately 13 million saying they did not know about privacy controls or had never set them. It says, "Facebook and other social networks collect enormous amounts of highly sensitive information."[47] This information includes names, phone numbers, birth dates, places and times that users have logged in, and lists of their friends. In addition, says *Consumer Reports*, even if Facebook users are aware of how much information is being collected about them, they have little legal power to do anything because US online privacy laws are weak.

> "Facebook and other social networks collect enormous amounts of highly sensitive information."[47]
>
> —Consumers Union, a nonprofit organization that works to ensure a fair and safe marketplace for consumers.

Personal Social Media Pages Influence Hiring Decisions

Many people consider the use of personal social networking pages in hiring decisions a violation of privacy. Despite this view, many job recruiters and human resources (HR) professionals report that they research potential job applicants online—including looking at social networking sites—and that their decisions are influenced by the information found there. Surveys such as this one from Cross-Tab research reveal that the practice is widespread. For this survey, researchers interviewed people in France, Germany, the United Kingdom, and the United States.

Percentage of recruiters and HR professionals who use these types of sites when researching applicants	
Search engines	78%
Social networking sites	63%
Photo and video sharing sites	59%
Professional and business networking sites	57%
Personal websites	48%
Blogs	46%
News sharing sites (e.g. Twitter)	41%
Online forums and communities	34%
Virtual world sites	32%
Websites that aggregate personal information	32%
Online gaming sites	27%
Professional background checking services	27%
Classifieds and auction sites	25%
None of these	2%

Source: Cross-Tab, "Online Reputation in a Connected World," January 2010. www.cross-tab.com.

Critics argue that social networking sites continue to push the boundaries of what is acceptable, collecting more and more information about users—gradually eroding their privacy. The site that has attracted most of the criticism in terms of privacy is Facebook. Writer James Cowan argues that despite statements from Facebook's creator that the website is designed to promote openness, Facebook is really motivated by self-interest—and that involves taking away privacy. He says, "Since its founding in 2004, it has prodded and cajoled people into making their information more public, forcing online culture to conform with its own corporate interests."[48]

Facebook makes most of its money selling ads on its websites, and by collecting user data it allows advertisers to better tailor those ads to consumers. Additionally, third-party developers who produce the games and quizzes that many Facebook users participate in are not bound by the same privacy rules as the social networking site. These third parties can collect a person's data without that person even playing—simply if a friend is playing—unless the person specifically opts out of this in privacy settings. The upshot of this is that social networking has already brought about a loss of privacy. Cowan says, "Whether or not we like it, the battle over privacy has already been fought. Facebook won."[49] He argues that Facebook has become such an important part of people's social lives that they will not give it up, even in the face of significant privacy concerns.

In 2012 Facebook introduced a new feature called Timeline, and this format prompts users to share even more information about themselves. It also organizes that information in a way that is easy to analyze—for Facebook friends and also for marketers. For example, users can tag posts according to their location or correlate them with life events such as getting married, getting a new job, or buying a car.

Far from Private

Social networks encourage users to post a lot of personal information online, and many people who engage in networking believe they are only sharing with their friends. However, once that information is put online, it is far from private. Numerous people, including friends of friends, potential employers, and marketers, have the ability to view the information posted on social networking pages. Social networking makes too much private information available to the public, and it is a threat to privacy.

Social Networking Is Not a Threat to Privacy

"It is a myth that social media companies are to blame for [threats to privacy]."

Lothar Determann, "Social Media Privacy: A Dozen Myths and Facts," *Stanford Technology Law Review*, July 10, 2012. http://stlr.stanford.edu.

Consider these questions as you read:

1. What do you think is meant by the argument that society is learning to view privacy in a different way?
2. Do you think social network users who fail to use privacy settings are at fault when their privacy is infringed on? Why or why not?
3. Mark Zuckerberg, creator of Facebook, has often argued that there are many benefits to openness and sharing on social networks. Do you agree or disagree with his point of view? Explain.

Editor's note: The discussion that follows presents common arguments made in support of this perspective, reinforced by facts, quotes, and examples taken from various sources.

As social networking becomes an important part of life, society is learning to view privacy in a different way. Social networking is not threatening privacy; instead, it is helping people learn that they do not need the type of privacy they thought they did. It is true that individuals who engage in social networking have less privacy in terms of who can see their personal information, and the majority are aware of this. For example, in a 2011 research study conducted for MSNBC.com by the Ponemon Institute, researchers found that 66 percent of social networkers agree that they have less control over their personal information than they did five years ago. However, the same study showed that frequent users of social networks are also far less concerned about privacy, despite the fact that some of their personal information is becoming increasingly public.

Bob Sullivan of MSNBC.com reports that only 14 percent of avid social networkers are more concerned about privacy in 2012 than they were five years ago: "Consumer behavior shows, repeatedly, that people just don't care about privacy."[50]

In 2010 software engineer Gary LosHuertos conducted an experiment that strongly supports this conclusion. He sat in a New York Starbucks coffee shop and hacked into the Facebook accounts of a number of people who were using the nonsecure free wireless connection there. LosHuertos used the victims' own Facebook accounts to send them messages warning that he had hacked into their accounts and knew where they were. However, many people did not seem to be worried. Even after receiving a second warning message from LosHuertos, some simply continued their Internet browsing over the nonsecure connection. One even shopped at Amazon.com. As this experience reveals, many people are surprisingly unconcerned about their privacy.

> **"Consumer behavior shows, repeatedly, that people just don't care about privacy."[50]**
>
> —Bob Sullivan, a technology correspondent for news website MSNBC.com.

Enabling Society's Desire to Share

Such research shows that society's definition of privacy is changing and that an increasing number of people have become comfortable with the fact that much of their online activity, including their social networking behavior, is being viewed by people they do not know. One example of social networking activity being tracked by strangers is the way Facebook collects large amounts of personal information for advertising purposes. While some people are uncomfortable with Facebook knowing so much information about them, others now believe it actually improves their networking experience. For instance, blogger Robert Scoble says, "I make everything public on my Facebook account and I'm not worried about privacy because the more I share about who I am and what interests me, the more Facebook can bring me content that I care about."[51]

As Scoble's comment reveals, social networking is not forcing people to be more open—it is simply enabling them to be if they want to be. Large numbers of people are embracing social networking because they want to be more open. Thus, it is not threatening their privacy, because they choose to participate in sharing their information.

The Benefits of Being Open

By adjusting the definition of privacy and choosing to share personal information, society can enjoy the many benefits that come with openness. Proponents of openness argue that by publicly sharing their lives on social networks, people increase their ability to learn new things and to make new connections and relationships. Journalist Jeff Jarvis argues, "If we become too obsessed with privacy, we could lose opportunities to make connections in this age of links."[52] Jarvis explains that connections only come with openness. He says, "To make connections, we must be public and share. To join up with fellow diabetics or vegetarians or libertarians or *Star Trek* fans, we first have to reveal ourselves as members of those groups. It's the same in the digital world as the real one: If you stay in your room all day, you'll never meet anyone and never know what you've missed."[53]

> "If we become too obsessed with privacy, we could lose opportunities to make connections in this age of links."[52]
>
> —Jeff Jarvis, journalist and author of *Public Parts: How Sharing in the Digital Age Improves the Way We Work and Live.*

Transparency and Accountability

The openness that comes with social networking increases transparency and accountability—which is a good thing. When people are more transparent, or open, with others about who they are and what they think, they create more honest and more fulfilling relationships. In addition, by giving up anonymity and interacting as their true selves, they are also more accountable for what they say. Before the creation of social networking, it was common to post things anonymously on the Internet. Technology expert David Kirkpatrick says, "There was hardly anywhere on the public Internet where you had to operate with your real name."

However, he says, on a social network, "You must have the courage of your convictions."[54] Because network users usually operate under their real identities, they are accountable to their friends for their words and actions, meaning that users are less likely to make thoughtless or unkind remarks.

Mark Zuckerberg, creator of Facebook, has often said that this is one of his goals in creating Facebook: to create a more open and transparent society. He says:

> The idea that my roommates and I talked about all the time was a world that was more open. We believed that people being able to share the information they wanted and having access to the information they wanted is just a better world: People can connect better with the people around them, understand more of what's going on with the people around them, and understand more in general.[55]

Sheryl Sandberg, chief operating officer of Facebook, argues that the more people share on social networks, the more authentic their online interactions will be. As Facebook prompts people to share more information about themselves—for example, by adding more details to their online profiles and sharing information about their online purchases or the music they listen to—they will be creating a more authentic online identity. Sandberg says, "Expressing our authentic identity will become even more pervasive. . . . Profiles will no longer be outlines, but detailed self-portraits of who we really are, including the books we read, the music we listen to, the distances we run, the places we travel, the causes we support, the videos of cats we laugh at, our likes and our links." Sandberg argues that while some people may fear that the sharing of so much information threatens privacy, they will eventually see that it actually enriches their online experience. She says, "Yes, this shift to authenticity will take getting used to and will elicit cries about lost privacy. But people will increasingly recognise the benefits of such expression."[56]

Privacy Is Not a Big Concern for Many Social Networkers

The widespread use of social networking is changing the way people view privacy. A survey of six hundred men and women in the United States reveals that many of the respondents do not feel threatened by sharing large amounts of personal information on their social networking pages. According to the survey, significant percentages of both men and women are willing to share personal details such as their email address, birthdate, personal photos, education, and occupation on their social networks.

Question: Are you willing to show:

Information	Gender	Yes	Probably not	Definitely not
Your name	Men	86%	10.3%	3.6%
	Women	88%	9.7%	2.2%
Your email address	Men	55.2%	32.9%	11.9%
	Women	42.4%	41.3%	16.4%
Your relationship status	Men	74.6%	15.9%	9.5%
	Women	72.5%	19.3%	8.2%
Your personal photos	Men	60.7%	23.8%	15.5%
	Women	50.9%	29.7%	19.3%
Your birthdate	Men	53.2%	23.8%	23%
	Women	46.1%	27.9%	26%
Your education	Men	72.2%	17.5%	10.3%
	Women	62.1%	27.5%	10.4%
Your occupcation	Men	66.7%	20.2%	13.1%
	Women	58.4%	27.1%	14.5%

Source: uSamp, "INFOGRAPHIC: uSamp Datapoint Study Finds Gender Gap over Social Media Privacy," January 30, 2012. http://blog.usamp.com.

Personal Responsibility

The real threat to privacy in relation to social networking is not the networks themselves, but irresponsible users. Many users threaten their own privacy by posting too much information about themselves and by not using available privacy controls. Social networks have privacy settings that allow users control over whom they share information with. For example, Facebook users can allow anyone to view their photos and comments, or they can restrict this content to only their friends or even to specific friends. By using these settings to control their information, users can greatly minimize the chance of someone invading their privacy. Yet many surveys show that a large number of people fail to protect their personal information with privacy controls.

In addition, some users share too much personal information. By posting excessive amounts of personal detail, they are eroding their own privacy, and in some cases sharing information that others can use in undesirable ways. For example, *Consumer Reports* says, "Our projections suggest that 4.8 million people have used Facebook to say where they planned to go on a certain day (a potential tip-off for burglars) and that 4.7 million 'liked' a Facebook page about health conditions or treatments (details an insurer might use against you)." *Consumer Reports* suggests, "Think before you type."[57]

Overblown Fears About Data Collecting

While social networks do collect data about their users for advertising purposes, in this they are no different than any of thousands of other websites that also collect user data. Fears about the way this data is used are greatly exaggerated. Online privacy expert Lothar Determann asks, "Where is the harm? All that advertisers want is to display more relevant advertisements to consumers. That in itself is hardly a bad thing. Relevant advertisements are better than irrelevant advertisements."[58]

Although consumers might not like to be the targets of sales pitches, advertising provides the income that many websites need in order to exist. Determann says, "Advertisers need tracking information to target ads, and social media companies need funding from advertisers in order to offer services free of charge to consumers. Without advertising dollars, Internet companies could never have created all the services that we have come to enjoy and depend on in our daily lives, including web search, maps and social media."[59]

A Better Online Experience

Social networking is changing society's definition of privacy, teaching people that they do not have to be afraid of openly sharing their thoughts and actions online. This openness is resulting in more genuine and more fulfilling experiences and has been eagerly embraced by most of society. Any threats to privacy come primarily from users who fail to use privacy controls or to exercise restraint in what they post on social network pages.

Chapter Four

Does Social Networking Threaten Teen Safety?

Social Networking Threatens Teen Safety

- Online predators use social networks to hide their true identities and to target vulnerable teens.
- Cyberbullying through social networks is a serious problem and can have devastating consequences for teens.
- Online bullying is often crueler and more harmful than bullying that occurs in person.
- Research shows that negative experiences on social networks are common among teens.

The Debate at a Glance

Social Networking Does Not Threaten Teen Safety

- Social networking has not increased bullying among teens.
- The media overemphasizes the role networking plays in teen suicides and other tragic events.
- Teens have become increasingly knowledgeable about how to use social networking safely.
- Parents are to blame for not educating teens about social media and not monitoring teens' online activity.

Social Networking Threatens Teen Safety

"Children and adolescents are at some risk as they navigate and experiment with social media."

Gwenn Schurgin O'Keefe, Kathleen Clarke-Pearson, and Council on Communications and Media, "Clinical Report—the Impact of Social Media on Children, Adolescents, and Families," *Pediatrics*, March 28, 2011. http://pediatrics.aappublications.org.

Consider these questions as you read:

1. Why do you think predators are able to successfully exploit teens through social networks?
2. Do you agree with the argument that online bullying can be crueler than offline bullying? Why or why not?
3. Taking into account the facts and ideas presented in this discussion, how persuasive is the argument that social networking can facilitate cyberbullying? Which facts and ideas are strongest, and why?

Editor's note: The discussion that follows presents common arguments made in support of this perspective, reinforced by facts, quotes, and examples taken from various sources.

Online predators frequently use social networks to target youth. Using networks allows them to pretend to be whoever they want, easily learn personal information about their victims, and target many youth at once. While the majority of social networks require users to provide their real names, it is easy to create a false identity, and false identities on social networks are fairly common. In 2012 Facebook reported that approximately 83 million of its user accounts were false or duplicate accounts. Because of the ease of using a false name, most predators interact online with fake names and made-up personal details. A common strategy for predators is to access teens' social networking pages in order to find personal information and then use this information to exploit those youths. Such information is easy to find, because teens routinely post all kinds of personal details on their social networking pages, and many do not use the appropriate settings to keep it private. Adam Mikrut is the founder of DigitalStakeout, a program used to monitor social networking sites for signs of predators. He says that by looking at a teen's social networking page, "I can understand who you are, what you like and what you value—and attain that information very quickly."[60] Not only is it easy for predators to contact and exploit teens, their actions often go undetected for a long time. This happens because in many cases, teens are reluctant to tell their parents about suspicious or disturbing online experiences because they are worried that their parents will restrict their online access.

> "[By looking at your social networking page] I can understand who you are, what you like and what you value—and attain that information very quickly."[60]
>
> —Adam Mikrut, founder of DigitalStakeout, a program used to monitor social networking sites for signs of predators.

Targeting Teens

There are numerous cases of predators using social networks to target teens. In 2011 fifty-three-year-old William Ainsworth of Pennsylvania was arrested and charged with using fake Facebook profiles to solicit nude photos and sex from underage girls. Prosecutors say that Ainsworth targeted girls with personal problems and used fake Facebook profiles to create a relationship with them. According to Pennsylvania attorney general Linda Kelly:

> What we found was an intricate web of false Facebook identities that were used to establish online relationships with vulnerable girls, who were then manipulated into sending nude photos to Ainsworth—believing he was a young surfer living in Florida— or physically meeting Ainsworth for sex—under the impression that those sexual encounters would help raise money so the girls could run away to Florida to be with their new online friend.[61]

Ainsworth was charged with sixty-eight felony accounts. In another case thirty-one-year-old Christopher Patrick Gunn of Alabama pleaded guilty in 2012 to producing child pornography with the aid of social media. Using fake profiles, Gunn made contact with hundreds of teenage girls and talked them into sending him sexually explicit pictures of themselves. One of his schemes involved befriending girls online and gaining their trust. He would then engage in intimate conversations with them, coaxing them into revealing details such as their bra size or their sexual history. Gunn would later threaten to reveal these conversations to others if the girls did not send him nude pictures.

Cyberbullying

Another way that social networking threatens teen safety is through cyberbullying. Cyberbullying is bullying that takes place online, commonly on social networking sites, and is a serious problem for teens. According to the American Academy of Pediatrics, it is the most common risk for youth on social media. The academy says, "Cyberbullying is quite common, can occur to any young person online, and can cause profound psychosocial outcomes including depression, anxiety, severe isolation, and, tragically, suicide."[62] In 2011 twelve-year-old Leslie Cote from Issaquah, Washington, was the victim of cyberbullying. After Cote got into an argument with two classmates, prosecutors say these two girls used Cote's password to post sexually explicit content on her Facebook page. They also sent messages to other users inviting them to her house to have sex. Both Cote and her parents were shocked when they found out. Cote says, "I was hurt and sad and very angry. . . . I kept crying the whole time."[63]

> "Cyberbullying is quite common, can occur to any young person online, and can cause profound psychosocial outcomes including depression, anxiety, severe isolation, and, tragically, suicide."[62]
>
> —American Academy of Pediatrics, an organization dedicated to the health and well-being of youth.

The two bullies received court sentences for their actions, but this did not undo the harm done to Cote. As her experience shows, cyberbullying can be devastating to teens. In some cases it has even led to suicide. In 2010 fifteen-year-old Phoebe Prince, a high school student in Massachusetts, committed suicide after being bullied by classmates, much of which occurred through Facebook. Prince was reportedly harassed by older girls at her school who were angry that she had dated a football player there. According to Massachusetts northwestern district attorney Elizabeth Scheibel, "The investigation revealed relentless activity directed toward Phoebe, designed to humiliate her and to make it impossible for her to remain at school." In the opinion of Scheibel, "The bullying, for her, became intolerable."[64]

Some researchers point out that because social networking involves online interaction instead of actual face-to-face interaction, bullying can be crueler and more harmful. Cyberbullies do not witness in person the effects of their bullying, so in many cases they do not see exactly how much it hurts the person it is directed at. Freelance writer and university student Sarah Zay says, "Deliberately insulting someone has become easier and more vicious than ever before. Kids tend to be more explicit in their insults when posting online, because there is no one physically present to confront their behavior."[65]

The Cyberbullying Research Center argues that one reason cyberbullying is difficult to prevent is because members of society generally do not take action to identify it and stop it as soon as it occurs. The center argues that schools are often reluctant to get involved because much of the bullying takes place outside of school, law enforcement does not become involved until there is clear evidence of a crime, and parents often lack the technical skills to monitor their children's online behavior. In addition, says the center, many people simply do not realize that cyberbullying is a serious problem. "As a result, cyberbullying incidents often slip through the cracks. Indeed, the behavior often continues and escalates because they are not quickly addressed."[66]

Formspring

Formspring is a website that has received a lot of attention for its connection to cyberbullying. This website allows users to post questions about themselves, and friends can anonymously post answers and comments. Critics argue that such anonymity makes bullying easy. Formspring users

Online Bullying Is a Problem

Online bullying is a significant problem, as this chart shows. The chart is based on 2012 research of youth in twenty-five countries, including the United States. It reveals that more than half of those surveyed know about online bullying and are worried about it. More than a third say they have actually been bullied online.

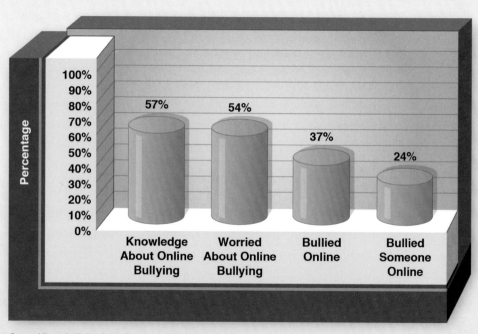

Online Bullying Metrics: Worldwide Averages

Source: Microsoft, "Online Safety Research," 2012. www.microsoft.com.

admit that much of the conversation on the website is unkind. The *New York Times* calls it "the online version of the bathroom wall in school, the place to scrawl raw, anonymous gossip."[67] New York City high school student Ariane Barrie-Stern has used the networking site, and she agrees that many users make mean comments about other people. "Nice stuff is not why you get it," she says. However, she adds, "I think it's interesting to find out what people really think that they don't have the guts to say to you. If it's hurtful, you have to remind yourself that it doesn't really mean anything."[68]

Yet not all users find it so easy to ignore the hurtful comments, and Formspring has caused serious harm to users as a result of the bullying that occurs there. Responding to an online article about the website, Trisha says, "Im 14 years old and i had an account i received over 30 anonymous people a DAY telling me to kill myself. i attempted to do so and was put in a hospital for a month. this site is just another way of letting cruel people talk to you."[69]

Troubling Experiences Are Common

While research about teen use of social networking shows that the majority of teens report networking to be a positive experience, it also reveals that a significant number of teens also have negative experiences. The Pew Research Center reports that teenage users of social networking sites are more likely to have negative experiences. Its 2011 study shows that 22 percent of teenagers have ended a friendship because of things that happened on social networking sites, 25 percent have had a face-to-face argument, and 8 percent have gotten into a physical fight. According to the Pew study, 20 percent of teens report that "people are mostly unkind" on social networking sites. The Cyberbullying Research Center reports that, based on its 2010 research of more than forty-four hundred students in the United States, about 20 percent have been victims of cyberbullying at one time in their lives.

Leslie Cote and Phoebe Prince are just two of the many hundreds of teens who have been harmed, either physically or mentally, as a result of social networking. This media makes it easier than ever before for predators or bullies to target teens. It is a threat to teen safety with the potential to cause serious harm.

Social Networking Does Not Threaten Teen Safety

"The Internet actually helps teens mature by allowing them to connect with others, learn and even advocate for a better world. . . . We should be thankful when kids go online, not afraid."

Rahul Parikh, "Our Overblown Paranoia About the Internet and Teens," *Salon*, May 16, 2011. http://salon.com.

Consider these questions as you read:

1. Some people argue that excessive media attention to cyberbullying makes it seem like a much larger problem than it really is. Do you agree or disagree with this argument? Explain.
2. Do you agree with the argument that parents are to blame for problems such as predation and bullying because they do not educate and monitor their teens? Explain.
3. How persuasive is the argument that if people under age thirteen were legally allowed to join Facebook, they might be safer? Explain.

Editor's note: The discussion that follows presents common arguments made in support of this perspective, reinforced by facts, quotes, and examples taken from various sources.

Social networking does not threaten teen safety. Every year an increasing number of teens use social media; however, research shows that they are in no more danger from threats such as bullying and predation than in the past. For example, a 2010 study in the *Archives of Pediatric and Adolescent Medicine* shows that both bullying and sexual victimization of teens has actually decreased in recent years. Between 2003 and 2008 physical bullying dropped from 22 to 15 percent, and emotional bullying from 25 to 22 percent. In 2012 Dan Olweus of the University of Bergen in Norway made a presentation at the American Psychological Association's annual convention, where he stated that cyberbullying is much less of a problem than many people believe. According to Olweus, "There is very little scientific support to show that cyberbullying has increased over the past five to six years."[70] In fact, in one study he found that an average of 18 percent of students reported being verbally bullied, and only 5 percent said they had been bullied online.

Danah Boyd, who researches youth and social media, argues that although there is a common public perception that social networking threatens teen safety, there is simply no data to support this. Boyd and others argue that the public merely believes this is true because there has been so much media focus on the topic of bullying. Says Boyd, "Every day, I wake up to news reports about the plague of cyberbullying. If you didn't know the data, you'd be convinced that cyberbullying is spinning out of control." However, she says, "the funny thing is that we have a lot of data on this topic, data dating back for decades. Bullying is not on the rise and it has not risen dramatically with the onset of the internet."[71] According to Boyd, most bullying actually takes place at school, not in social networking forums.

Social Media Is Not the Cause

In recent years there have been a number of widely publicized stories about tragic events that have occurred in connection with social networking. One example is Phoebe Prince, the Massachusetts student who committed suicide in 2010 after repeated bullying. However, the news media often distort the reality of these situations. Although bullying through social networking may have played a role in some suicides, the media often overemphasize this factor, overlooking other problems, such as severe depression. Journalist Katherine Bindley argues that many teens who have committed suicide after bullying already had serious mental health problems and that these problems may have been the real cause of the suicides, not the bullying. Ann Haas, with the American Foundation for Suicide Prevention, agrees. She says, "Years and years of research has taught us that the overwhelming number of people who die by suicide had a diagnosable mental disorder at the time of their death."[72]

Journalist Emily Bazelon researched the Phoebe Prince case, doing extensive interviews and reviewing law enforcement records. She found a more complicated story than the one reported by the news media, revealing that Prince had emotional difficulties and had been cutting herself since 2008. Bazelon does not discount the harm that the bullying caused, but she also believes Prince's mental health played a role in her suicide. She maintains, "Her death was tragic, and she shouldn't have been bullied. But she was deeply troubled long before she ever met the six [accused bullies]."[73]

Bullying and predation can occur anywhere, and although they do occur through social media, this medium is not the cause of the problem. As technology expert Paul Shirey explains, "Social Media . . . [is] just another medium at which some bullies choose to do what they please. People who have never touched Facebook still get bullied."[74]

As social networking becomes an increasingly common part of life, teens are actually becoming more knowledgeable about how to use it safely. One study supporting this was conducted in 2010 by cyberbullying experts Sameer Hinduja and Justin W. Patchin. They examined teen use of the social network MySpace. The researchers found support for their hypothesis that teens have become more knowledgeable about how to protect themselves while engaging in social networking. Specifically, the researchers found that 85 percent of users restricted access to their profile in 2009, compared with only 39 percent in 2006. They also found that in 2009 teens were less likely to post personal and private information to their public MySpace profile than they were in 2006.

> "Social Media . . . [is] just another medium at which some bullies choose to do what they please. People who have never touched Facebook still get bullied."[74]
>
> —Paul Shirey, a technology expert and founder of the blog *Paul Shirey Tech.*

Parents Are the Problem

When problems such as bullying or predation of teens do occur through social networking sites, much of the blame lies with parents, not the social network. Many parents are at fault for not educating their children about responsible media use and for not monitoring their children's social networking activities. If children are not educated about responsible media use, they will never learn how to avoid the potential dangers of social networking. Edward Christophersen, a clinical psychologist at Children's Mercy Hospital & Clinics, advises, "The most important thing a parent can do is set expectations for the child's privilege of using e-mail, text and social media tools, and then monitor, monitor, monitor."[75]

Yet research shows that many parents do not educate or monitor their children. According to Stefanie Thomas, from the Internet crimes section of the Seattle Police Department, many parents have no idea what their children are doing on the Internet. She says, "This is a huge issue in this area and all around the country, the disconnect between what parents think their kids are doing online, and then, in turn, what their children are actually participating in."[76]

A 2012 report by Internet security company McAfee supports this argument. McAfee found that 71 percent of teens have done something to hide their online behavior from parents, and only 56 percent of parents are aware of this. Significant numbers of those teens surveyed admitted to visiting a website that parents disapproved of or accessing nude photos or porn online. One in three of those parents surveyed reported that they feel helpless to keep up with their teens' online behavior because they lack the technical knowledge. McAfee insists, "Parents must be jolted out of their complacency. A huge gap exists between what teens are doing online and what parents really know. Parents must take an active role to ensure their teens are practicing safe online behavior."[77]

> "This is a huge issue in this area and all around the country, the disconnect between what parents think their kids are doing online, and then, in turn, what their children are actually participating in."[76]
>
> —Stefanie Thomas, a victim advocate for the Internet crimes section of the Seattle Police Department.

A Surprising Difference

Gisella Larson is the mother of a nine-year-old. She shares an experience in which there was a surprising difference between what she thought her son was doing online and what was really occurring. According to Lar-

61

Cyberbullying Has Not Increased with Social Networking

Fears of increased teen cyberbullying resulting from social networking are overblown. The dramatic increase in the number of youth engaging in social networking has not seen a corresponding rise in cyberbullying. According to a comparison of seven different studies, cyberbullying rates have fluctuated over time but show an overall decrease between 2004 and 2010. This result suggests the absence of a correlation between social networking and cyberbullying.

Lifetime Cyberbullying Victimization Rates
Seven Different Studies 2004–2010

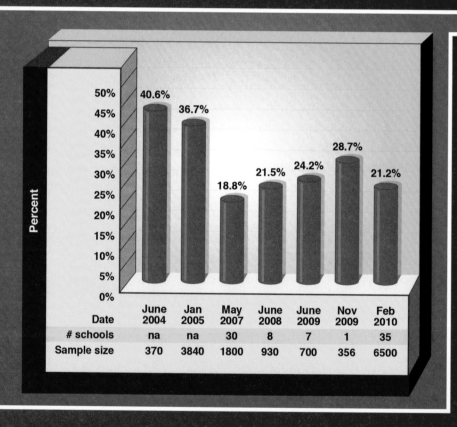

Date	June 2004	Jan 2005	May 2007	June 2008	June 2009	Nov 2009	Feb 2010
# schools	na	na	30	8	7	1	35
Sample size	370	3840	1800	930	700	356	6500

Source: Sameer Hinduja and Justin W. Patchin, "Cyberbullying: Identification, Prevention, and Response," 2010. www.cyberbullying.us.

son, her son was using Instagram, a photo-sharing application. But she was shocked to find out that her son was definitely not using Instagram the way she thought he was. She explains:

> My 9 year old son signed up for . . . [Instagram] on his iTouch and I thought it was a camera program like CamWow. Two days into his account, I see it blinking at night so I go to check it out. It was a message from a 32 year old woman on Instagram contacting my son. On top of that, my son had been having conversations with a 50 year old man. Further investigation led us to pictures my son had seen. PORN.[78]

In the case of younger children, many are not only unmonitored by their parents, they are on sites not intended for their use. For example, Facebook, the most commonly used social network, requires users to be at least thirteen years old. In a 2012 survey of 2,179 Americans, Children's Mercy Hospitals & Clinics found that 68 percent of parents agree that children should be aged thirteen or older to join Facebook. Yet research shows large numbers of underage children with Facebook accounts. *Consumer Reports* estimates that approximately 5.6 million children under age thirteen have Facebook accounts. Some people argue that society needs to acknowledge the reality that young children are using sites such as Facebook so that steps can be taken to make their experience safer.

Not a Significant Danger

Teens can be at risk for bullying, predation, and other dangers anywhere they go, and social networks are no exception. However, social networking is not the cause of these problems and is not making them worse. As in all aspects of life, parents need to educate and guide their teens to help keep them safe.

Source Notes

Overview: Social Networking

1. Kaitlin Kerry Eckrote, "The Best Addiction Ever: Facebook," *Science in Our World: Certainty & Controversy* (blog), Pennsylvania State University, October 11, 2010. www.personal.psu.edu.
2. ComScore, "It's a Social World: Top 10 Need-to-Knows About Social Networking and Where It's Headed," 2011. www.comscore.com.
3. ComScore, "It's a Social World."
4. Quoted in Vito Pilieci, "Canadian Group Studies Impact of Social Networks on Mental Health," *Montreal Gazette*, March 24, 2012. www.montrealgazette.com.
5. Sherry Turkle, *Alone Together: Why We Expect More from Technology and Less from Each Other.* New York: Basic Books, 2011, p. 161.
6. David Kirkpatrick, *The Facebook Effect: The Inside Story of the Company That Is Connecting the World.* New York: Simon & Schuster, 2010, pp. 200–201.

Chapter One: Does Social Networking Benefit Society?

7. Billygean, "Social Networking—More Connected than Ever—a SPN Exclusive Article," *Social Networking* (blog), SiteProNews, May13, 2011. www.sitepronews.com.
8. Zeynep Tufekci, "Social Media's Small, Positive Role in Human Relationships," *Atlantic*, April 25, 2012. www.theatlantic.com.
9. Quoted in Robert Fine, *The Big Book of Social Media: Case Studies, Stories, Perspectives.* Tulsa, OK: Yorkshire, 2010, p. 263.
10. Sheryl Sandberg, "Sharing to the Power of 2012," *Economist*, November 17, 2011. www.economist.com.
11. Kirkpatrick, *The Facebook Effect*, p. 7.
12. Wael Ghonim, interviewed by Steve Inskeep, "Social Media Advances 'Revolution' in Egypt," NPR, January 17, 2012. www.npr.org.
13. Josh Rose, "How Social Media Is Having a Positive Impact on Our Culture," Mashable, February 23, 2011. http://mashable.com.

14. Rose, "How Social Media Is Having a Positive Impact on Our Culture."

15. Turkle, *Alone Together*, p. 156.

16. OffPiste, comment on *Economist*, "*Economist* Debates: Social Networking," February 16, 2012. www.economist.com.

17. Denise Morris, "Facebook—Where Everybody Knows Your Opinion," *The Boundless Line* (blog), April 2, 2012. www.boundlessline.org.

18. Quoted in Common Sense Media, "Social Media, Social Life: How Teens View Their Digital Lives," Summer 2012. www.commonsense media.org.

19. Quoted in Common Sense Media, "Social Media, Social Life."

20. Stephen Marche, "Is Facebook Making Us Lonely?," *Atlantic*, May 2012. www.theatlantic.com.

21. Sherry Turkle, "The Flight from Conversation," *New York Times*, April 21, 2012. www.nytimes.com.

22. *New Media Age*, "Is Facebook's Banishing of Anonymity a Good Thing?," March 10, 2011, p. 5.

23. Connie Schultz, "The Lonely World of Facebook," *Shelby Star* (Cleveland County, NC), April 15, 2012. www.shelbystar.com.

24. *Evolution of Thoughts* (blog), "Kony 2012: Social Awareness or Social Group-Think?," March 8, 2012. http://evolutionofthoughts.com.

25. Marche, "Is Facebook Making Us Lonely?"

Chapter Two: Does Social Networking Have a Positive Impact on the Individual?

26. Quoted in Ruth Spencer, "Facebook and Loneliness: Our Readers Respond," *Guardian* (Manchester, UK), April 20, 2012. www.guardian .co.uk.

27. Pew Research Center, "Pew Internet: Social Networking (Full Detail)," March 29, 2012. http://pewinternet.org.

28. Common Sense Media, "Social Media, Social Life."

29. SarahMummy, "Better at Writing than Talking," *Mum of Three World* (blog), August 9, 2012. http://mumofthreeworld.blogspot.com.

30. Danika Gusmeroli, comment on Danaleong, "Social Networking Provides Opportunities for Teenagers to Develop Social Skills Online," CommUnity: Online Conference on Networks & Communities, April 25, 2012. http://networkconference.netstudies.org.

31. Karen Ballum, "Using the Internet to Find Your Community," *BlogHer*, October 25, 2012. www.blogher.com.

32. Matt Britland, "Social Media for Schools: A Guide to Twitter, Facebook, and Pinterest," *Teacher Network* (blog), *Guardian* (Manchester, UK), July 26, 2012. www.guardian.co.uk.

33. *The World Unplugged* (blog), "Going 24 Hours Without Media," 2011. http://theworldunplugged.wordpress.com.

34. Matt Richtel, "Attached to Technology and Paying a Price," *New York Times*, June 6, 2010. www.nytimes.com.

35. Richtel, "Attached to Technology and Paying a Price."

36. Jene, comment on *Every College Girl* (blog), "4 Reasons to Delete Your Facebook and Never Look Back," July 17, 2012. http://every collegegirl.com.

37. Susan Dominus, "Underage on Facebook," *Redbook*, January 2012. www.redbookmag.com.

38. Jenna Wortham, "PING; Feel like a Wallflower? Maybe It's Your Facebook Wall," *New York Times*, April 10, 2011. www.nytimes.com.

39. Dominus, "Underage on Facebook."

40. Turkle, *Alone Together*, p. 172.

41. Quoted in Turkle, *Alone Together*, p. 175.

Chapter Three: Is Social Networking a Threat to Privacy?

42. Quoted in Kathiann M. Kowalski, "Protect Your Privacy Online: Keep Personal Information Private for Your Own Good!," *Current Health Teens, a Weekly Reader Publication*, December 2001. www .weeklyreader.com.

43. Jenna Wortham, "The Facebook Resisters," *New York Times*, December 14, 2011. www.nytimes.com.

44. Quoted in Wortham, "The Facebook Resisters."

45. *Consumer Reports*, "Facebook & Your Privacy: Who Sees the Data You Share on the Biggest Social Network?," June 2012. www.consumer reports.org.

46. Mark Sullivan, "Data Snatchers! The Booming Market for Your Online Identity," *PCWorld*, June 26, 2012. www.pcworld.com.

47. *Consumer Reports*, "Facebook & Your Privacy."

48. Quoted in Kenneth Partridge, ed., *Social Networking*, New York: Wilson, 2011, p. 130.

49. Quoted in Partridge, *Social Networking*, p. 129.

50. Bob Sullivan, "Why Should I Care About Digital Privacy?," MS-NBC.com, March 10, 2011. www.msnbc.msn.com.

51. Quoted in *Consumer Reports*, "Facebook & Your Privacy."

52. Jeff Jarvis, *Public Parts: How Sharing in the Digital Age Improves the Way We Work and Live*. New York: Simon & Schuster, 2011, p. 5.

53. Jarvis, *Public Parts*, p. 45.

54. Kirkpatrick, *The Facebook Effect*, p. 292.

55. Mark Zuckerberg, interviewed by Fred Vogelstein, "The *Wired* Interview: Facebook's Mark Zuckerberg," *Wired*, June 29, 2009. www.wired.com.

56. Sandberg, "Sharing to the Power of 2012."

57. *Consumer Reports*, "Facebook & Your Privacy."

58. Lothar Determann, "Social Media Privacy: A Dozen Myths and Facts," *Stanford Technology Law Review*, July 10, 2012. http://stlr.stanford.edu.

59. Determann, "Social Media Privacy."

Chapter Four: Does Social Networking Threaten Teen Safety?

60. Adam Mikrut, "Sex Predators Target Children Using Social Media," *USA Today*, March 1, 2011. www.usatoday.com.

61. Quoted in Pennsylvania Attorney General, "Attorney General Kelly Announces Criminal Charges in Elaborate 'Facebook' False Identity Scam Targeting Young Girls for Sex," February 10, 2012. www.attorneygeneral.gov.

62. Gwenn Schurgin O'Keefe, Kathleen Clarke-Pearson, and Council on Communications and Media, "Clinical Report—the Impact of Social Media on Children, Adolescents, and Families," *Pediatrics*, March 28, 2011. http://pediatrics.aappublications.org.

63. Quoted in John Discepolo, "Facebook Bullying Victim: 'I Kept Crying the Whole Time,'" KOMO News, April 26, 2011. www.komonews.com.

64. Quoted in Russell Goldman, "Teens Indicted After Allegedly Taunting Girl Who Hanged Herself," ABC News, March 29, 2010. http://abcnews.go.com.

65. Sarah Zay, "What Sticks & Stones Can't Do Facebook Will—and More!," *USA Today*, March 2011. www.usatoday.com.

66. Sameer Hinduja and Justin W. Patchin, "Cyberbullying: Identification, Prevention, and Response," Cyberbullying Research Center, 2010. http://cyberbullying.us.

67. Tamar Lewin, "Teenage Insults, Scrawled on Web, Not on Walls," *New York Times*, May 5, 2010. www.nytimes.com.

68. Quoted in Lewin, "Teenage Insults, Scrawled on Web, Not on Walls."

69. Trisha, comment on Mary Kate Cary, "Nothing Good Can Come of Formspring, Cyberbullying's Newest Venue," *U.S. News & World Report*, May 6, 2010. www.usnews.com.

70. Quoted in American Psychological Association, "Cyberbullying Less Frequent than Traditional Bullying, According to International Statistics," August 4, 2012. www.apa.org.

71. Danah Boyd, "The Power of Fear in Networked Publics," 2012. www.danah.org.

72. Quoted in Katherine Bindley, "Bullying and Suicide: The Dangerous Mistake We Make," *Huffington Post*, February 8, 2012. www.huffingtonpost.com.

73. Emily Bazelon, "What Really Happened to Phoebe Prince?," *Slate*, July 20, 2010. www.slate.com.

74. Paul Shirey, "Does Social Media Cause Bullying?," *Paul Shirey Tech* (blog), January 14, 2012. http://paulshireytech.com.

75. Quoted in "Social Media Is Parents' Friend, Not Enemy, New Report from Children's Mercy Hospital and Clinics Finds," Children's Mercy Hospitals & Clinics, August 16, 2012. www.childrensmercy.org.

76. Stefanie Thomas, interviewed by Drew Pinsky, "Teen Love Triangle Explodes on Facebook; Cyberbullying on the Internet," transcript, CNN, April 21, 2011. http://transcripts.cnn.com.

77. McAfee, "The Digital Divide: How the Online Behavior of Teens Is Getting Past Parents," June 2012. www.mcafee.com.

78. Gisella Larson, comment on Mary Kay, "Instagram—Is It Okay for Kids? What Parents Need to Know," *Yoursphere* (blog), February 8, 2012. http://internet-safety.yoursphere.com.

Social Networking Facts

Who Uses Social Networking

- Based on a study of 2 million people in 171 countries, research company comScore found that in 2011 people in Israel spent the most time on social networking sites, an average of more than 11 hours a month, followed by Argentina at 10.7 hours and Russia at 10.4 hours.
- The Pew Research Center reports that in 2011, 64 percent of adults in the United States reported using social networking sites.
- In the United States, social networking is most common among people aged eighteen to forty-nine, according to the Pew Research Center.
- Common Sense Media, an organization that works to educate families about the media they consume, reports that three-quarters of American teenagers belong to a social networking site and more than a third of them visit it several times a day.

Most Popular Social Networks

- In a 2011 survey of 2,260 adults in the United States, the Pew Research Center found that Facebook was the most commonly used site, with 87 percent of social networking users having a Facebook profile; 14 percent used MySpace, 11 percent used Twitter, and 10 percent used LinkedIn.
- Research company A.C. Nielsen reports that Americans spend more time on Facebook than they do on any other website.
- According to statistics released by comScore in February 2012, Pinterest had more than 10 million monthly unique visitors and was the third-most popular social networking site, behind Facebook and Twitter.

Teen Harm Online

- The organization WiredSafety reports that more than 50 percent of cyberbullying is conducted anonymously.

- In 2012 *Consumer Reports* estimated that of the approximately 5.6 million children under age thirteen with Facebook accounts, about 800,000 had experienced harassment or cyberbullying.
- According to a 2012 report by Internet security company McAfee, only 49.1 percent of parents had installed parental controls on their computers, and 44.3 percent knew their teens' passwords. Only 21.7 percent of parents thought their teens could get in trouble online.
- According to the Pew Research Center, based on 2011 surveys of both teens and adults, 12 percent of teens and 7 percent of adults report that they frequently see mean behavior on social networking sites.
- According to a 2012 survey of youth aged eight to seventeen in twenty-five countries, 50 percent of parents had talked with their children about online risks.

Negative Effects

- According to a 2012 survey of 1,003 twelve- to seventeen-year-olds by the National Center on Addiction and Substance Abuse at Columbia University, 75 percent of those surveyed said that seeing pictures of teens partying with alcohol or marijuana on social networking sites makes other teens want to party in the same way.
- According to a 2010 report by market research company Cross-Tab, 70 percent of US recruiters and human resources professionals had rejected job candidates on the basis of data they found online, such as that posted on social networking sites.
- Common Sense Media reports that, according to a 2012 survey of thirteen- to seventeen-year-olds in the United States, 44 percent of those who use social networking sites strongly agree that social networking often distracts them from people they are with.
- According to a 2011 survey of 2,337 adults by the National Cyber Security Alliance and security company McAfee, 15 percent of Americans had never checked their social networking privacy settings.

Positive Effects

- In a 2012 survey of 2,179 Americans, Children's Mercy Hospital & Clinics found that 83 percent of parents believed the benefits of social media use outweighed the risks.
- According to a 2012 report by the Pew Research Center, social networking is primarily a positive experience for users. The center found that 85 percent of adults using social networking sites say people are mostly kind.
- According to the Pew Research Center, about two-thirds of social networking users say they use such sites to stay in touch with family members and current friends. Half report that an important reason they use the sites is to connect with old friends.
- In 2011 the Pew Research Center, the Family Online Safety Institute, and Cable in the Classroom surveyed 799 youth aged twelve to seventeen and their parents. Surveyors report that 65 percent of those teens using social media have had an experience on a social networking site that made them feel good about themselves.

Related Organizations and Websites

Avoid Facebook

4 Robert Speck Pkwy., Suite 1500, Mississauga, ON Canada L4Z 1S1

website: www.avoidfacebook.com

Avoid Facebook is a group dedicated to promoting safe and responsible use of social networking. It provides numerous articles intended to help educate people about the potential dangers of using social networking sites like Facebook.

Center for Safe and Responsible Internet Use

474 W. Twenty-Ninth Ave.

Eugene, OR 97405

phone: (541) 556-1145

e-mail: contact@csriu.org • website: www.cyberbully.org

The Center for Safe and Responsible Internet Use works to help young people keep themselves safe and respect others on the Internet. Its website has numerous reports and guides designed to help people learn about responsible Internet behavior.

Common Sense Media

650 Townsend St., Suite 435

San Francisco, CA 94103

phone: (415) 863-0600 • fax: (415) 863-0601

website: www.commonsensemedia.org

Common Sense Media is an organization that believes the media have a profound influence on youth. It was created in order to help educate families about media, including social networking, and to give them the information and tools they need to make educated choices about their media use.

Cyberbullying Research Center
website: www.cyberbullying.us

The Cyberbullying Research Center is a clearinghouse of information about cyberbullying. It provides information about the nature, extent, causes, and consequences of cyberbullying among teens. The website contains numerous statistics about this issue and stories from youth who have been affected by cyberbullying.

Electronic Frontier Foundation (EFF)
454 Shotwell St.
San Francisco, CA 94110-1914
phone: (415) 436-9333
e-mail: information@eff.org • website: www.eff.org

The EFF is a nonprofit organization founded in 1990 that seeks to defend various civil liberties in relation to telecommunications technologies such as the Internet. Its website has information about free speech and privacy issues related to social networking.

GetNetWise
e-mail: cmatsuda@neted.org • website: www.getnetwise.org

GetNetWise is a website provided by Internet industry corporations and public interest organizations. Its goal is to ensure that Internet users have safe and constructive online experiences. The website contains information for both youth and parents about social networking, youth safety, security, and privacy.

Internet Society (ISOC)
1775 Wiehle Ave., Suite 201
Reston, VA 20190-5108
phone: (703) 439-2120 • fax: (703) 326-9881
e-mail: isoc@isoc.org • website: www.internetsociety.org

The ISOC is an international nonprofit group that works to ensure the open development of the Internet for the benefit of people throughout the world. Its website contains information about social networking and privacy issues.

Pew Internet & American Life Project

1615 L St. NW, Suite 700

Washington, DC 20036

phone: (202) 419-4500 • fax: (202) 419-4505

e-mail: info@pewinternet.org • website: http://pewinternet.org

The Pew Internet & American Life Project studies how Americans use the Internet and how digital technologies are shaping the world today. Its website has the results of numerous studies on social networking.

WiredSafety

website: www.wiredsafety.org

WiredSafety is a nonprofit group that was founded in 1995. It works to educate people of all ages about online safety. Its website provides information about numerous safety issues, including cyberbullying and privacy.

For Further Research

Books

Jeff Jarvis, *Public Parts: How Sharing in the Digital Age Improves the Way We Work and Live*. New York: Simon & Schuster, 2011.

David Kirkpatrick, *The Facebook Effect: The Inside Story of the Company That Is Connecting the World*. New York: Simon & Schuster, 2010.

Kenneth Partridge, ed., *Social Networking*. New York: Wilson, 2011.

Bonnie Szumski and Jill Karson, *Is Social Networking Beneficial to Society?* San Diego, CA: ReferencePoint, 2013.

Sherry Turkle, *Alone Together: Why We Expect More from Technology and Less from Each Other*. New York: Basic Books, 2011.

Jim Whiting, *Online Communication and Social Networking*. San Diego, CA: ReferencePoint, 2012.

Deanna Zandt, *Share This! How You Will Change the World with Social Networking*. San Francisco: Berrett-Koehler, 2010.

Periodicals

Consumer Reports, "Facebook & Your Privacy: Who Sees the Data You Share on the Biggest Social Network?," June 2012.

Susan Dominus, "Underage on Facebook," *Redbook*, January 2012.

Economist, "Facebook and Children: Let the Nippers Network," June 9, 2012.

Stephen Marche, "Is Facebook Making Us Lonely?," *Atlantic*, May 2012.

Matt Richtel, "Attached to Technology and Paying a Price," *New York Times*, June 6, 2010.

Sherry Turkle, "The Flight from Conversation," *New York Times*, April 21, 2012.

Internet Sources

Common Sense Media, "Social Media, Social Life: How Teens View Their Digital Lives," Summer 2012. www.commonsensemedia.org.

ComScore, "It's a Social World: Top 10 Need-to-Knows About Social Networking and Where It's Headed," 2011. www.comscore.com.

Index

Note: Boldface page numbers indicate illustrations.